Y0-BRF-446

5 Minute AMAZING Animal Stories

Sarah Howden

Illustrated by Iris Tian

Collins

5-Minute Amazing Animal Stories
Copyright © 2019 by HarperCollins Publishers Ltd.
All rights reserved.

Published by Collins, an imprint of HarperCollins Publishers Ltd

No part of this book may be used or reproduced in any manner whatsoever
without the prior written permission of the publisher, except in the case
of brief quotations embodied in reviews.

5-Minute Amazing Animal Stories includes certain imagined elements in tales based on real events.

HarperCollins books may be purchased for educational, business,
or sales promotional use through our Special Markets Department.

HarperCollins Publishers Ltd
Bay Adelaide Centre, East Tower
22 Adelaide Street West, 41st Floor
Toronto, Ontario, Canada
M5H 4E3

www.harpercollins.ca

Library and Archives Canada Cataloguing in Publication
information is available upon request.

ISBN 978-1-4434-5813-9

Printed and bound in China
RRD/SC 9 8 7 6 5 4 3 2 1

Contents

THE SEEING-EYE CAT

Terfel was a brown Labrador retriever, and he was getting old. He'd had a good life, romping and playing outside and chasing the odd rabbit, but those days were done now. He was going blind.

Terfel had cataracts, a film that had developed over his eyes, a bit like clouds across the sun. This dog who used to be so lively was bumping into walls and doorframes, and he could no longer find his way home.

So Terfel made a decision: He would stay inside and stick close to his bed. That would be safe. Lonely, but safe.

Terfel listened as the cats in the house chased each other, and he smelled the delicious scents they carried in on their fur after wandering in the garden.

He missed his old life.

One afternoon, he smelled something
different—someone different. It was a
new cat. Not only could Terfel smell it,
he could hear it—hissing and squabbling
with the other cats. *I hope she doesn't pick
a fight with me*, he thought.

3

Just then, he heard the **click-click** of claws on the floor. The new cat was coming his way. Terfel scrunched down in his bed and pretended to be asleep. The other cats were watching, he could tell.

The new cat stopped just beside Terfel and leaned toward him—Terfel could feel her breath on his nose.

And then she gave him a lick . . . and started washing his face! Terfel was confused.

Slowly Terfel opened his eyes. Even with his dim vision, he could make out the form of this small feline, white and gray with hazel eyes. For some reason, the cat seemed to want to be friends.

Terfel blinked and gave the cat a lick back. Then he rose up onto his feet, tottering, and sniffed her. She smelled like a friend. The cat sauntered away, signaling for him to come along.

But Terfel couldn't go—it wasn't safe. He sighed and was about to sit back down when the cat nudged him. The purring creature weaved back and forth in front of him, as if telling him to follow, showing that she wouldn't go far.

Terfel wasn't sure.
His heart fluttered in fear.

But somehow, Terfel felt he could trust her.

So he took a step out of his bed. Then another. The cat stayed close, advancing a tiny bit at a time, looking back with each new step.

Slowly, very slowly, they moved across the room.

The other cats were astonished. Here was this scrapper of a cat being kind and gentle with, of all creatures, a DOG? It didn't make sense.

When the pair got to the door, the cat pushed it open and held it for Terfel.

He could see, by the splash of light, what the cat was doing. Terfel could tell she wanted him to come outside. Cautiously, Terfel moved forward. But then he hesitated.

What would Terfel do if the cat
left him alone out there?
He would have to get back
on his own, smacking his nose
into every obstacle on the way.
He could almost feel the bumps
and bruises now—*OUCH!*

But . . . here was the cat,
purring softly beside him,
wanting to help.

And wasn't life all about
making new friends and
snuffling along outside with
his nose to the earth?

And so Terfel went through the door. Quick as a flash, the cat was right in front of him, showing him where to walk. They took each step together, the cat pressed to his side.

"You've led him outside, have you?" came their owner's voice. "Well, aren't you a good pudditat!"

Pudditat (spelled Pwditat): The name stuck, and so did she.
The little cat had found her family, and Terfel had found a friend.

Terfel couldn't believe his luck. He had a sense that his life was changing, right then and there. That this cat was going to help him go places, help him to not be afraid. She was going to be his eyes and guide him around, snuggle with him, and play with him.

Terfel found a spot in the garden and started digging with all his might. He had missed this feeling.

He was a happy dog again.

BELUGA BUDDIES

Neville couldn't say exactly when he'd gotten lost. It might have been when he'd gone to check out that shipwreck. Or when he'd raced after that colorful fish that turned out to be a leaf.

All he knew was that he wasn't in Baffin Bay anymore.

When Neville's parents had agreed to let him go exploring alone, they'd made him promise to stick to the well-known routes. And he'd meant to. But sometimes he just had to follow his tusk, even if it meant getting off track.

Now he wasn't sure what to do. He imagined what his parents would say . . .

"Swim on," said his father's voice. "Eventually, you'll get your bearings."

Neville tried that for a while . . . but nothing looked familiar. Maybe that trick only worked when you were close to home.

"Stay calm, and keep a lookout for orcas,"
his mother's voice said. "They love a narwhal snack!"

Neville surfaced and scanned the area for the black-and-white whales. Was that one on the horizon, its fin cresting the water?

Frantically, Neville dove back down and swam away, fast. When he spotted an opening, he took it. It was a river of some sort, with land rising on either side.

Now he was definitely in uncharted waters.
He was seeing creatures he'd never seen before . . .
and they were seeing him.

Schools of strange fish swam around him,
gawking at his tusk.

One fish called out "Nice horn!" before
swimming off. Neville knew she didn't mean it
nicely.

He felt a shiver go from tusk to tail. He was the only narwhal these animals had ever seen, which meant he didn't belong here. And that he was in danger. A lone narwhal, out of his element, would be the perfect prey.

I'm going to get eaten! he thought. *I'm all alone and I'm going to get eaten!* Desperately, he surfaced and scanned the waterline for the dreaded orcas.

Was that a dorsal fin? No, just the crest of a wave. And the occasional jumping fish.

And—what was this?—a pod of teenaged beluga whales, splashing and chasing each other in a sort of gleeful whirlwind.

A whirlwind that was coming his way! Before he could move, one of the whales ran smack into Neville, knocking him sideways.

"Watch out!" Neville said, but he didn't really care. He was alone, with no friends and no place to call home. What did it matter if he got pushed around?

"Sorry!" said the whale. Then he paused and gazed at Neville. Neville was sure he was going to make fun of his tusk, or maybe tell him to scram. Instead, the whale smiled and said, "Do you want to play with us?"

Neville was confused. He looked at the belugas, plunging after each other, squeaking with delight, and then back at the whale in front of him.

"My name's Joe," the whale said.
"I'm Neville."
He thought for a moment. *What about finding his way home? What about watching for orcas?*

But again, he could hear his mother's voice in his head: "Never pass up a chance to make new friends."

And so he said,
"Yes. Yes, I'd love to play!"

Soon, Neville was jumping and swimming with the energetic creatures, playing and scuffling just like he was a beluga. All his fears had melted away. It was as if he were back home, with his friends. And no one seemed to mind that he was different.

That night, Neville met the belugas' pod. "Stay as long as you like!"
said Joe's mom, beaming. "And when you're ready, Joe can help you
find your way home."

For the next few days, Neville had a blast. The whales treated him like one of their own, and he and his new friends wore themselves out playing tag and wrestling and chasing fish.

Finally, when it was time to go, Neville said his goodbyes, and Joe swam by his side to the Labrador Sea.

"I know the way from here," said Neville. "And thank you. For everything."
"Come back anytime!" said Joe, giving a big wave as Neville swam away.

The rest of Neville's journey went by in a flash, as he remembered all the fun times he'd had and how being lost had turned into the greatest adventure of his life. Neville knew he had traveled to a place no narwhal had ever been, which was pretty incredible.

But his very favorite part was meeting his new beluga friends.

BUDDY LEADS THE WAY

Ben Heinrichs was working in the shed beside his family's home. It was getting cold, so he had a heater on to keep himself toasty. And he had his friend Buddy, the German shepherd, by his side.

"Thanks for helping me fix my truck," Ben said, giving the dog a pat. It wasn't a bad way to spend an evening. They liked each other's company.

Everything changed in an instant. The heater threw a spark into a puddle of gas in the corner, and suddenly the building was on fire.

Ben ran out, shutting the door behind him to contain the flames.

"Oh no!" he cried, realizing Buddy was still inside. He darted back to throw the door open, and Buddy came bounding out.

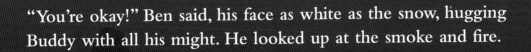

"You're okay!" Ben said, his face as white as the snow, hugging Buddy with all his might. He looked up at the smoke and fire.

"We need help, Buddy. We need help now."

Buddy looked at Ben for a long moment. Then he jumped up and ran off into the woods. Ben didn't blame him; he was a timid dog.

Ben dashed toward his house to warn his parents and call for help. Luckily, someone already had.

Across the way, Ben's neighbors had looked out their window to see a ball of flame shooting into the sky. They'd called 911 to report the emergency.

State trooper Terrence Shanigan heard the call. He was out in his car, not too far from the scene. Quickly, he punched the address into his computer so it would give him a map and show where to go.

"Come on," he said to the screen. Nothing was happening. It was black. Terrence tapped it with his hand. "Come on!" he urged again.

But he was out of luck. "Of all the times to break . . . ," Terrence muttered.

The country roads outside Anchorage, Alaska, twisted and turned every which way, across fields, through woods, over ditches. Even the people who lived out there didn't know all the shortcuts.

Terrence sighed and turned his car around, speeding toward the area of the fire. How he would find the house, he wasn't sure.

The trooper squinted into the darkness, hoping to catch sight of
the light from the flames so it might help guide the way.

But what was that, at the corner up ahead? A coyote? He
turned up his headlights, and in the darkness he saw a dog.
A German shepherd. Standing there, alert.

It was as if the animal was waiting for him. The trooper slowed down, and the dog came trotting up to the car. It looked him right in the eye, and then turned and started to run.

Terrence had a lot of experience with dogs. He knew exactly what Buddy was doing—Buddy wanted him to follow.

Quickly, he jerked the steering wheel, and the car spun around the corner. Buddy was galloping along as fast as he could,

Sometimes the dog would look back to check that he was still there and then take a turn onto the next road. Every time Terrence was unsure of where to go, Buddy was there, urging him in the right direction.

Three turns they took, getting farther and farther into the country.

"Where are we?" Terrence asked, peering around. He shook his head, wondering if he'd made a mistake. Maybe the dog was simply a stray, leading him to the middle of nowhere.

Just then, he rounded a final corner . . . and saw flames lighting up the night. The fire—he had found it!

"Arf! Arf!" Buddy barked, as if making sure Terrence understood.

"I've got it, pup," Terrence said, nodding at the dog. "And thank you!"

He made a call on his radio. "I'm at the Heinrichs' house," he said. "I can guide fire and ambulance here. It's way out in the backwoods."

He looked over at Buddy. If the dog hadn't been there, he might never have found the place.

When the fire truck arrived to put out the flames, Ben and his parents were safely out front with Trooper Shanigan. Buddy stood by their side.

The firefighters did the best they could. The shed was ruined, but thanks to Buddy, the house was saved. A little singed, but saved.

Later that night, the family sat inside at their kitchen table, drinking hot chocolate. Buddy lay on the floor at their feet.

"What a dog," Ben said, and they all turned to look at Buddy. "What would we do without him?"

But Buddy didn't hear their praise. He was fast asleep.
After all, he'd had a hard night. He deserved a good, long rest.

BEAU AND BEATRICE

Beatrice was always up before Beau in the morning, nickering at him until he awoke.

But today, all had been quiet until the farmers, Jane and Donald, arrived. When Beau blearily opened his eyes, he couldn't see Beatrice. And neither could they.

"Beatrice!" Jane said, rushing over to the mare's stall.

"She's collapsed," Donald said, opening the stall door. "It looks like colic."

"Beatrice needs to stand up. We've got
to get her back on her feet," Jane said.
"Otherwise she could die."

Horses aren't meant to lie down, at least not for long.
The longer she stayed on the floor, the sicker she
would get.

As Jane and Donald strained to lift Beatrice up,
Beau looked on, helpless.

Jane tried to let him out to eat his breakfast, but he wouldn't budge. Normally Beatrice was the first one to the feeder for meals. She'd gobble down the freshest hay before Beau could even get settled. But she always stayed by his side until he was finished. Without her, he wasn't hungry.

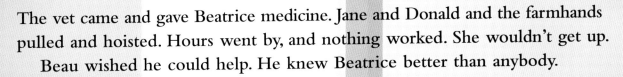

The vet came and gave Beatrice medicine. Jane and Donald and the farmhands pulled and hoisted. Hours went by, and nothing worked. She wouldn't get up. Beau wished he could help. He knew Beatrice better than anybody.

"If this keeps up, she won't last much longer," Donald said. It was afternoon now, and the winter sky was already beginning to darken.

Then Jane snapped her fingers. "The tractor!" she said. "We'll haul her to her feet!"

She and Donald hurried to the other side of the stable and returned with some straps, which they fastened around Beatrice. Then they lowered a strap through a trapdoor in the roof and clipped it on.

Outside, Beau could hear the tractor roaring to life. "Ready!" Jane called. The strap tightened as the tractor pulled, and Beau could hear Beatrice shifting in her stall.

"That's it, that's it . . . ," Donald said. *Please*, Beau thought. *Please.*

The tractor stopped. Jane came in, looking hopeful. But Beau saw Donald shake his head. "I'll call the vet," he said, wiping away a tear.

Beau knew what came next. He knew the vet would take Beatrice away, and that she would not come back. He was going to lose his best friend.

What would he do without her? Who would he race to the far fence with, or buck and play with, or graze side by side with, smelling the breeze?

"Time for some fresh air, old boy," said Donald sadly. Beau looked down to see his stall door open. This was his chance.

Instead of trotting out into the pasture, he made his way over to Beatrice.

"Uh, Beau . . . ," Jane began. But she and Donald stood back and let him lean over the stall door. At first, he just nuzzled Beatrice softly. Then he nipped at her ears. Beatrice snuffled, but she didn't move.

Beau nudged her harder and started biting at the scruff of her neck. She grunted back.

This was it, Beau thought. This was Beatrice's last chance. His last chance.

Planting his feet, he took a deep breath, bit down on her halter as hard as he could, and heaved with all his might. He pulled and pulled, his neck muscles bulging, his whole body straining against the weight.

Beatrice's hooves splayed out, sliding and kicking against the stall wall as her body lifted off the ground. Would she just fall back down again?

Then there was a gasp from Jane and Donald . . . Beatrice was doing it.

She was standing up. Wobbling, but upright.

Beads of sweat rolled down her nose as she swayed there, legs shaking but holding fast. The mare blinked at Beau. It was a thank-you. He gave her a gentle nip.

I won't let you fall, he was saying. *I promise.*

Jane and Donald were speechless. After all their efforts, it was Beau, their horse, who had found the solution. Beau had saved Beatrice's life.

A little while later, when Beatrice was ready, Beau walked by her side out into the yard. She was a bit slower than usual, her gait a little less sure, but she still found the energy to trot ahead and beat Beau to the water trough. She was going to be just fine.

ONE STRONG SWIMMER

It was December 1919 when the SS *Ethie* set off from Cow Head, Newfoundland, with its passengers and freight. The sky was dark, but Captain Edward English decided to depart anyway. He wanted to make it back home before Christmas.

Soon his mistake was clear. A blizzard descended. Snow and ice pellets lashed the ship, raging winds tore everything off its decks, and the sailors tried desperately to keep the vessel afloat.

We won't survive out here, thought the captain. *But there's no safe place to dock. Unless we want to sink, we'll have to run aground!*

Running aground meant steering the ship into shallow water. It was a last-ditch effort to get close to land. And any mistakes could be deadly.

"You called for me, Captain?" It was Walter Young, the ship's purser. "I hear you grew up on this coast," the captain said. "I need your help. Where can we beach the ship close by?"

Walter studied the ship's chart. "There's a reef near here," he said, pointing to the map. "From there we can rig up a rope to get people to safety."

The captain gave his orders and the crew turned the ship toward the coastline. Soon after, the *Ethie* shuddered and groaned as it beached itself on the reef.

"Captain, we're taking on water!" a crewman called. The ship's hull had been ripped open by the jagged rocks.

Some people on the shore had spotted the ship and gathered to help, but in between them and the *Ethie* were the rough waters of the sea.

"How will we get the rope across?" Walter asked.

"We have to find our strongest swimmer," the captain said. His eyes settled on a figure padding confidently across the tilting deck. It was Tang, the ship's dog.

Tang ran over and licked the captain's hand. "Tang is a water dog," the captain said. "He once helped rescue a man from rough seas."

He crouched beside Tang and put his hand on the dog's back. "What do you think, friend? It's a dangerous job."

"Woof!" the dog said, wagging his tail.

The captain stood up and nodded at Walter. "We'll have to try."

Walter gave Tang the end of the rope. "Take this across to shore," he said. Just then, the ship gave a lurch.

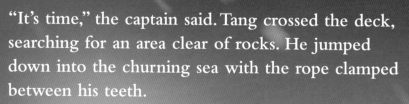

"It's time," the captain said. Tang crossed the deck, searching for an area clear of rocks. He jumped down into the churning sea with the rope clamped between his teeth.

"If he's struggling, throw him the life preserver," the captain told Walter. And they watched as the tiny dog bobbed and sank in the enormous waves, his little legs propelling him forward.

People on shore had spotted Tang and were shouting and coaxing him on.

"He's doing it!" the captain said in wonder.

Just then a giant wave crested . . . and the dog disappeared.

Captain," Walter said, staring at the water. The snow was thick, and he rubbed his eyes to try to clear them. The captain peered down. He couldn't see Tang either. Only the blackness of the sea.

"Throw the life preserver!" he yelled. Walter readied to fling it into the waves when . . .

"HURRAH!" They heard the cheers from the shore.

Tang was clambering up on land, soaked, but alive and well.

A man took the rope from the dog, tied it tightly to a huge rock, and soon the line was ready for its cargo. Now came another difficult task.

One by one, the sailors and passengers made their way over, dangling above the roaring sea. There was a baby on board, so they nestled her into a mailbag and fed it across. Everyone held their breath until she made it to the other side, into her mother's arms.

It was slow, tense work, but eventually everyone made it to solid ground. All ninety-two people were saved.

"Good dog, Tang," the captain said, leaning down to give him a pat. "Very good dog."

The next day, the newspapers reported the ship's close call—but only some mentioned the dog's part in the rescue. Some say he was a fiction, added in later to make the story that much more colorful.

Yet not long afterwards, the community raised money for a special tribute: a silver-plated collar for a dog from that very ship.

Stamped into the front?

The word *hero*, in block letters.

WILLIE'S NEW WORD

Willie the parrot was a pretty smart bird. That is, he was pretty and he was smart.

His plumage was multicolored and glorious.

And his brain was always on. With a quick mind like his, Willie needed to keep himself busy. Sometimes he would gather small objects he found around the house and make a nest. Sometimes he would sit and chew on things. And sometimes he would talk.

Boy, did he like talking. It didn't matter if anyone was listening.

Mostly, he spoke parrot. It was his first language, after all. But his owner, Megan, had taught him some English. He could say *Mama* and *hello* and *bye-bye*, and he was hoping to add to that list.

Some people think parrots just mimic words—copy
the sounds people make—but that wasn't true for
Willie. He understood them too. When Megan said,
"Please stop chewing that" and "Willie, did you steal
my socks again?" and "Dinnertime!" he knew what
she meant.

Willie wished he could say more. Sometimes he even practiced saying words by himself at night, when it was just him and the moon. It was hard, but he liked trying to get his tiny parrot tongue to make new sounds.

He was working on a new word now, in honor of Hannah. *Baby.*

Hannah was one of Willie and Megan's roommates—she and her mom, Samantha, shared the apartment with them. Hannah was two years old and she loved Willie. She would watch him chatter, clap her chubby little hands, and laugh. Willie liked putting on a show for her.

Sometimes when Samantha went out, Megan and Willie would look after the baby. And she needed a lot of looking after. She couldn't say very many words herself, and she was always toddling around, grabbing things she shouldn't.

One morning, Megan and Willie were on babysitting duty. **Pop!** went the toaster, and Willie tried imitating it—"Pop!"—but he couldn't get it quite right. Megan buttered a piece of toast for Hannah and then ducked out to the bathroom. Hannah sat in front of the TV, munching away.

A few moments later, Willie noticed something was wrong.

First, Hannah seemed oddly quiet. Then she started coughing and sputtering. And her face changed from pinkish to white to . . . blue.

A face wasn't supposed to be blue. Willie knew that.

He needed to tell Megan right away. But what could he do to show he wasn't just playing? He would have to try out his new word.

Quickly, Willie winged his way to the bathroom, where Megan was washing her hands. He fluttered and flapped, squawking, "Mama, baby! Mama, baby!"

Megan had never heard Willie say *baby* before . . . "Hannah!" she shrieked.
She rushed to the other room and found the girl choking. Willie watched as Megan wrapped her arms around Hannah and squeezed, to try to dislodge the food.

It didn't work the first time. Willie flapped and fluttered. He clacked his beak in distress.

Megan tried again. One, two, three—heave! A piece of food came flying out of Hannah's mouth.

Cough, cough, cough. Hannah sputtered and gasped. But her face was going back to its normal pink! She was breathing again!

Willie was so happy, he flew around the room, squawking with joy.

"She's okay!" Megan cried, her eyes welling up. "You're okay," she whispered to Hannah, giving her a long hug.

Willie flew over to perch on Hannah's hand and she gazed at him.

"Baby," Willie said with relief. Hannah smiled and chuckled. Then she turned back to the TV.

"Thank you, Willie," Megan said, wiping the tears from her face. "Thank you so much."

Willie wanted to say, "You're welcome" and "I'm so glad she's okay" and "I love Hannah" and "I love you," but he didn't know how. He just blinked back at her as she stroked his feathers. It didn't matter, though: Megan knew what he felt, and this time, Willie didn't have to say a word.

A GENTLE GIANT

Michael was three years old, and he loved to run. Today they were at the zoo, and his mother, Emily, kept saying, "Hold my hand!" But off he'd go anyway, with her chasing after him.

So far they'd visited the kangaroos, the giraffes, and the rhinos, and now they were going to see the gorillas. But where had Michael gone?

Emily was rushing around, searching for a glimpse of his blond hair, when she heard someone yell, "NOOO!" A few people screamed. What had happened? And why was everyone staring into the gorilla pit?

She pushed her way through the crowd to look over the railing. There, on the ground, was Michael. He was lying still, as if he were asleep.

"MICHAEL!" she cried. "Help! That's my son! Somebody help!"

A zoo worker raced up. Her nametag said *Jade*. "I've called the emergency team," she said. "They're on their way." Emily stood frozen in place, watching the gorillas gather around her son.

"They'll hurt him!" someone said.

Even though they look a bit like people, gorillas are wild animals. Most of these creatures had never seen a kid up close before, so no one knew how they would behave. It was possible they might think he was a toy. Or a dangerous animal.

A female gorilla stepped toward the boy. She had her own baby clinging to her back.

"That's Binti," Jade said quietly. Emily's stomach lurched. *What am I going to do?* she thought.

Binti leaned in toward Michael and stroked his cheek with her finger. His eyelids fluttered. She took a look at the others and then looked back at Michael. All at once, she scooped him up in her arms. Emily gasped.

Everyone watched nervously to see what Binti would do next. She was so big and strong.

"Binti was raised by humans," Jade said softly. "So I'm sure she doesn't mean harm. We're like family to her." Emily nodded. Her face was as white as paper.

Binti sat down and gathered Michael into her lap. She rocked him back and forth a bit, as if trying to calm him.

"Even though she never knew her parents, she's been such a good mother to her own baby," Jade said. "I think she knows that your boy is a baby too."

From behind them came the pounding of footsteps. "Team one, go to the enclosure door. Team two, get the hose," a zookeeper yelled. The emergency crew had arrived.

"Don't worry, ma'am. It won't be much longer," a zoo worker said. "We'll get your son."

"Turn it on!" another team member called. He began spraying a wall of water between Binti and the other gorillas. The animals edged back, not interested in getting wet.

"They're keeping the other gorillas away," Jade said, "to keep Michael safe."

Binti kept holding Michael, staring down at him. People had their cameras out and were taking photos. It was an incredible sight.

And then Binti shifted and stood up, with Michael cradled against her. She started carrying him across the enclosure.

"Where is she taking him?!" Emily said, grasping the railing, her knuckles white.

The door of the enclosure opened, and some zoo workers gathered inside. Binti was coming their way. As she got closer, the workers tensed up. Emily held her breath.

Binti walked up to the workers, looked them over, and then laid Michael down, very gently, at their feet. She stared at them a moment more before backing away, as if to say, "Here he is. Take care of him."

Just then, Michael stirred and opened his eyes. "He's waking up!" Emily shouted.

"I'll take you to him," Jade said, leading the way. As they arrived, Michael was being wheeled out on a stretcher.

"He has a broken hand and a few scratches, but he'll be just fine," said the paramedic. "We gave him some medicine for the pain."

Emily dove forward to give Michael a big hug and kiss. "Are you okay?!"
she asked. "You must have been so scared!"

Michael nodded. "I fell," he said. Then he glanced around and his eyes
lit up. "Mommy?" he said.

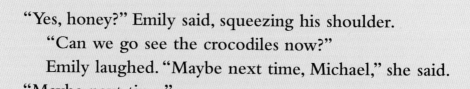

"Yes, honey?" Emily said, squeezing his shoulder.

"Can we go see the crocodiles now?"

Emily laughed. "Maybe next time, Michael," she said. "Maybe next time."

LULU, THE LIFE-SAVING PIG

When Jackie adopted the pot-bellied piglet, she was a tiny little thing. With her curly tail and wiry black hair, the creature weighed all of four pounds—about the same as a honeydew melon.

Jackie named the piglet LuLu, and she could tell right from the start that she was special.

Then something happened that was clearly meant to be: Jackie went away and left LuLu with her parents, Jack and Jo Ann. They weren't sure they could look after a pig, but LuLu fit right in. She got along well with their dog, Bear, and she curled up at the bottom of their bed at night.

When Jackie saw how happy LuLu was—and how much her parents loved her—she realized LuLu had found her forever home. Over the next year, that tiny piglet grew and grew and grew. After months of munching on potatoes and veggies and, her favorite, jelly donuts, she was 150 pounds— the weight of a full-grown person!

But no matter how big LuLu got, Jack and Jo Ann always had room for her. Even if space did get a little tight.

And so that summer, when LuLu was just over a year old, they all piled into the family truck and went on vacation to Presque Isle State Park. It was a lovely spot, with trees and water and plenty of fresh air.

This was where LuLu's life changed forever.

One sunny day, Jack went out fishing, leaving Jo Ann, Bear, and LuLu at home. As Jo Ann was making lunch, she suddenly fell to the floor, crying out in pain.

Bear was scared, and he barked and barked. And LuLu started to cry, her big teardrops splashing onto the floor.

But it didn't take her long to realize that Jo Ann couldn't get up. And crying and barking weren't going to help. She needed to do something.

LuLu knew there was only one way out: the dog door. A pig as big as LuLu wasn't meant to fit through that small a space, but she shoved and pushed and wrenched her way forward until, finally, she had made it outside.

She was cut and hurting from the tight squeeze, but that didn't matter now. She had to get someone's attention. It was a quiet morning, and no one was around. But there were cars on the road.

LuLu knew traffic was dangerous. But this was her only idea. She lay down, right in the middle of the road.

HONK! A car swerved and drove past her. The next car sped around her too, tires squealing. LuLu pressed her eyes shut in fear as a third car headed her way. She hoped this one wouldn't hit her.

But luck was on her side. The car slowed, pulled over, and stopped.
    LuLu heard a man's footsteps on the gravel—someone was coming toward her! *It's time*, she thought. She pushed herself up and started trotting away, praying the man would follow.

And he did.
All the way to the trailer.

"Hello?" the man called. "This pig needs help!" He peered around but couldn't see anyone.

And then he heard it. "I need help too!" came a voice through the window. "Call an ambulance!"

The man's mouth fell open.

He grappled for his phone and called 911. Soon after, the emergency crew arrived. They gathered Jo Ann up and sped off.

LuLu and Bear stayed behind, listening to the siren fade in the distance.

A few months later, there was LuLu: onstage at the Mayflower Hotel in New York. She was being awarded a gold medal for her brave deed. Everyone was clapping.

And by her side was Jo Ann, alive and well. Her collapse had been caused by a heart attack, and she had needed surgery at the hospital right away.

If another fifteen minutes had passed, the doctors said, she wouldn't have made it. LuLu had saved her life.

No matter that the medal was too small to fit over LuLu's head, or that a tuft of her black hair was sticking out the wrong way— when that medal was draped over LuLu's neck, she was one perfect pig. She was dignified and noble.

And she was a hero.

HUMPBACK HERO

"Good luck!" says Nan's friend Robert as she jumps off the boat into the calm waters. But she won't need it.

Nan has been studying whales for the past twenty-eight years. The ocean is like a second home to her, and the whales are like family. She's done this hundreds of times.

Nan spots a humpback whale and begins swimming toward it, just the way she always does. But suddenly, something strange happens. The whale turns and swims right at her.

This isn't normal.
Nan's never seen this before.

Nan has had some scary encounters with whales in the past.

A few times, the gigantic creatures have rammed up under the boat she was on and tried to push it over. And once, a female humpback launched herself up on deck, smacking right into Nan before splashing back down into the water.

But Nan has somehow never felt unsafe. Not until now.

The whale crashes into Nan, shoving her with its head and sending her tumbling backward. It takes her breath away, and the water swirls around her as she tries to keep control.

Relax, Nan tells herself. *Don't let it know you're scared.*
Even though her boat is nearby with her friend
Robert on board, there's nothing he can do. Right now,
it's just Nan, alone with a humpback as heavy as two
school buses. And it's pushing her around.

Nan crests above the water and gulps some air. But the whale is twisting around and swimming back already.

It rams Nan with its flank, blasting her sideways.

"Ow!" Nan cries. Her heart is thumping in her chest. This whale could hurt her.

Before Nan can figure out what to do next, the whale swims underneath her and lifts her onto its back.

She scrabbles against it with her hands, trying to get a grip, but it's too slippery. Nan just slides over the smooth skin and splashes back into the ocean.

She looks into the creature's enormous eye, as big as a grapefruit. *What is it?* she wants to ask. *What are you up to?*

Next, the whale sweeps up beside her. Its huge fin splashes down onto Nan, and she is pushed under and tucked against the whale's side like a teddy bear.

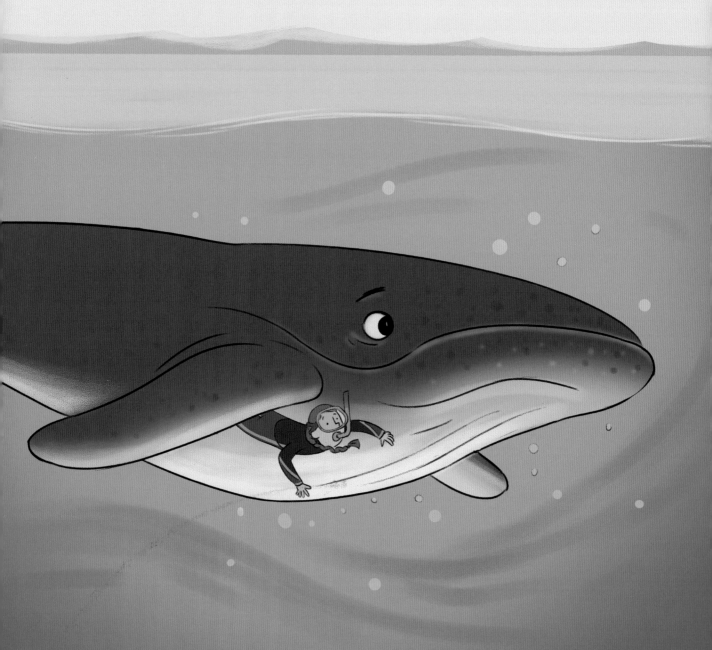

Nan breaks free and surfaces, gasping for air. Still, something tells her to stay calm. If she just keeps swimming, maybe she can make it back to her boat.

Again and again, the whale pushes Nan sideways, as if it's trying to move her somewhere. But where, and why? Nan keeps her eye on the boat, inching her way closer.

Finally, after what feels like hours, she makes it to the side of the vessel, and Robert is right there to haul her up onto the deck.

"I don't know what went wrong," Nan says, shaking her head. "I couldn't tell what was happening."

"There's something else out there," Robert says, pointing at the water. In the near distance, Nan sees a dorsal fin.

That's no whale . . .

"A shark," she says. "It's a tiger shark!" Tiger sharks are huge creatures with powerful jaws, and they will eat almost anything.

Suddenly, everything makes sense.

Robert looks at Nan. "Whales sometimes protect seals from sharks—"

"By tucking them under their fins!" Nan finishes, breaking into a grin. She can't quite believe it. All that time, the whale had been protecting her. Keeping her safe.

As if in answer to Nan's thoughts, the whale floats to the surface, shooting a stream of water out of its blowhole. The sound is like a huge fizzy drink exploding.

"Thank you!" Nan calls as the humpback plunges back into the water. "Thank you so much. I love you!"

The creature turns its big eye on Nan, as if checking to see that she is okay. Then, with a swish of its tail, it swims back out to sea.

TARA, THE CAT WARRIOR

Tara was just a little kitten, scruffy and skinny, when she followed Erica and Roger home from the park.

She was alone and needed a family. But not just any family—Tara had a good feeling about these folks. They had a good feeling about her too, and they took her in.

In her new home, Tara was safe and happy and loved. It was a dream come true.

Best of all, she had a new brother, a baby whose name was Jeremy. He was just a helpless little noodle, waving his arms and legs about, crying a lot. Tara knew what it felt like to be small and scared. She knew Jeremy needed her just like she'd needed his family.

She would sneak into Jeremy's bed and sleep beside him when he was napping. And she would purr when he gave her full-body hugs, even if he pulled her fur. She just liked being close to him.

As Jeremy grew older, Tara kept an eye on him, like any good big sister would. When he went tearing around the house chasing his brother, she'd sit close by and doze, keeping her ears perked up for trouble. If Jeremy was outside playing ball, she would lie in the grass, alert just in case.

He was a busy bee, but Tara didn't mind.

And so on one sleepy spring day, when Jeremy was playing on his bike in the driveway, Tara was nearby. Everything seemed quiet.

But next door, the neighbors had left their back gate open. And they had a new guard dog.

Most dogs are peaceful animals. But this dog hadn't been trained yet. He didn't understand kids, and when he heard Jeremy, the fur on his back stood up. Jeremy was on his turf.

132

The dog caught Jeremy's scent and raced out of his yard, growling. When he got close, he lunged and grabbed Jeremy's leg with his teeth. Jeremy shrieked as the dog yanked him down off the bike.

But Tara wasn't afraid. In a flash, she was hurtling toward the dog. He was a wiry creature, and she was so much smaller, not half as strong . . .

But Tara knew what to do. She leapt into the air, throwing her entire body sideways into the dog.

Jeremy heard a thud, and suddenly the dog went skidding down the driveway. Tara had given him a wallop, and he had barely landed on his feet. He went yipping off home with Tara right on his heels, hissing and snarling.

By the time Tara ran back to check on Jeremy, his mother was there. He was crying, but Tara knew his mom would take care of him. Still, she stood close by, ready to help.

After the ambulance whisked them off to the hospital, Tara stayed behind and worried.

Would Jeremy be okay? She sat by the door until finally she heard the key in the lock.

Tara's heart was thumping. First came Jeremy's mom . . . and then in walked Jeremy. He was all right! Tired, with a sore leg, but all right. The doctor had fixed him up wonderfully.

Tara mewed and rubbed against his good leg. She gave him lots of kisses and promised to stay near him and help him get better.

Everyone was so happy that Jeremy wasn't badly hurt. But his parents had to know what had really happened.

Gritting their teeth, they watched the security video, and that was when they saw the real story. A cat-shaped blur had zoomed in and defended their Jeremy.

They couldn't believe it.
Tara was a hero!

They gave Tara endless hugs and pets, and in the days to come, they told the incredible story to all their friends. Who would have thought their sweet little cat could fight off a tough guard dog?

Jeremy's dad put the footage up on YouTube, and suddenly the whole world was talking about Tara and her brave rescue.

Tara was famous. She got awards and appeared on talk shows. She even rode in a parade. And she deserved all of the glory.

But for her, the best times were still the simple ones: at home with her family. She had three little-boy brothers now, plus a dog sister, Maya, and she was fond of all of them.

Of course, Tara was still closest with Jeremy. They were best friends. Every day, she would wait outside for him to come home from school. Tara would always have his back.

SERGEANT RECKLESS

The gunfire came from everywhere. **BOOM!** A bomb exploded and dirt rained down. But no matter what, Reckless kept going. She had an important load to carry, and her platoon was depending on her.

Not long ago, she wouldn't have known what to do out there on the battlefield. The noise and commotion would have sent her running for cover. And she could run fast; she used to be a racehorse.

But her racing days were long behind her.
The war had come to Korea, the racetrack had
become an airstrip, and she had been sold to the
United States Marine Corps, which needed a
horse to carry heavy cargo.

It hadn't taken Reckless long to feel like part of the platoon. The marines had been so kind, and soon she was gobbling up scrambled eggs and pancakes with them at breakfast, sharing their rations of candy and cola after a tough day of training, and even joining them at poker games—munching on poker chips when the guys weren't looking!

She did love to fill her stomach. And the marines grew to love the plucky little horse who would eat just about anything.

Her closest friend was Sergeant Joseph Latham, who had trained her to do her new job. He'd helped her learn how to carry a load of heavy shells—ammunition that would explode when it hit a target. He'd shown her how to find her footing on the steep hills and rice paddy fields.

And, hardest of all, he'd helped her get used to the noise and danger of battle. It was like a different world out there, so loud and dizzying and scary.

Sometimes, it took everything Reckless had to just keep going. But she forced herself to be brave and strong.

Her friends were counting on her!

Now that she'd been doing this for months, she was good at it. But she still got nervous. Two days ago, when the enemy had attacked, she'd heard the explosions and huddled in her bunker, shivering.

"I know it's bad out there," Sergeant Latham had said. He stroked her neck and she felt calmer. "But this is an important fight, Reckless. We can't lose this ground. We really need you." He smiled, but Reckless knew he was afraid. They both were.

And they were right to be. This battle was the worst of the war so far. It seemed like it would never end.

Now, as she hauled another massive load of shells over the rocky terrain, the horse kept her head down. She had been working day and night.

"Thanks, Reckless," shouted Private Washington when she arrived. Quickly, he unloaded the shells. "We needed these." He patted her muzzle. "And Jake needs a doctor." He strapped the injured man to the horse's back. "Good luck."

And so Reckless traveled back and forth, back and forth, into battle with ammunition or away with injured soldiers. Sometimes when she got to the bunker, her friends would make her stop for a break: a drink of water, a bit of food, a quick nap. But soon she would be back out there, in the smoke and clamor.

The battle lasted three whole days. By the end, many soldiers had lost their lives. But the US Marines had not backed down. They had won.

"You saved lives out there, Reckless," Sergeant Latham said as they sat together in his tent. "You were very brave." Reckless whinnied. She knew he had been brave too. They all had.

But she didn't know just how big her part had been.

She didn't know how much it meant to the marines to see her out there plodding along, never giving up.

But Reckless didn't want to think about the battle. She had something else on her mind as Private Washington appeared in the doorway.

"Here it is," he said, waving a loaf of bread.

He and Latham slathered slices with strawberry jam, making two sandwiches. Then they passed them both to Reckless. She devoured them in seconds. The two men chuckled fondly.

Reckless had many more hard days ahead of her. She knew that. But it was all worth it—for these moments with friends, and for the hope that the war would end one day.

Eventually, at long last, the war did end—and Reckless made it through. In thanks for her service, the marines brought her back to America and awarded her two medals for her bravery. She retired at Camp Pendleton, in sunny California, where she was allowed scrambled eggs (with salt, no pepper) and sometimes even a cola.

Reckless got plenty of visitors too. Men from the war who had traveled great distances to see her. They wanted to say thank you, to give her a pat . . . and to tell their children:

"This is Sergeant Reckless. A magnificent horse, and one tough marine."

ELEPHANTS TO THE RESCUE

Ever since they'd come to the Thula Thula wildlife reserve, Nana's elephant herd had lived pretty well. The park was huge, so there was lots of room to explore. And they were safe from their biggest danger, hunters.

Which meant life was good, if sometimes a little boring.

"It's not that I liked being hunted, back in those days," said Nana to her friend Hortense as they went for a stroll. "But knowing there was danger did keep things interesting."

"True," Hortense said. They wandered over to a stand of acacia trees to grab a snack.

"But of course, life is better now," Nana said.

"Much better," Hortense replied, crumpling some leaves into her mouth.

A rumbling sounded in the distance.
As it grew louder, Nana and Hortense
ducked under the trees to hide.

"Helicopter!" Nana said, and the two elephants
watched as it hovered into view. In its path was a herd
of antelopes, running from the noise. To either side of
the panicked creatures were people with their arms
outstretched, herding them toward a pen.

As Nana and Hortense watched, the antelopes were funneled through the open gate and then locked inside. Job done, the helicopter disappeared, the people dispersed, and everything was quiet again. Almost as if nothing had happened.

Nana and Hortense stared at each other, their ears pricked up in excitement.

"They probably don't mean any harm to the antelopes," Nana said slowly.

Hortense nodded. "After all, the people here take care of us."

"But it's the principle of the matter," Nana replied. "Wild creatures are not meant to be penned."

"And so," said Hortense, with a twinkle in her eye, "we must stage a rescue."

Nana and Hortense had gathered up the elephant herd and presented their plan. Then, they'd waited until after sunset. And now, under cover of darkness, they were ready.

Stealthily, the herd crept across the land. It didn't take long for them to arrive at the pen. Inside were the antelopes, trapped against their will.

"Circle around!" Nana called, and the elephants spread out, taking their places around the walls to keep a lookout. No matter what the people were up to, they wouldn't be happy to lose their antelopes. And Nana and the herd didn't want to be captured themselves.

They would have to be careful. And quick.

Nana strode forward to examine the locks on the gate. There were three in all, made of solid metal, and she knew they wouldn't be easy to break. But her trunk was strong, and she was determined.

She chose one lock, gripped it with her trunk, and fiddled and pulled and twisted until . . . **CLANG!** Off it came.

"Hooray!" Hortense trumpeted.

"Shh!" Nana said.

"Hooray," Hortense whispered.

Nana began on the second lock. As the wind rose up, she paused. Was that the sound of an engine? She peered across the landscape, searching for headlights. Nothing. She continued.

CLANG! The second lock was done.

"Just one more," Nana muttered. This one was a different kind, though, and it was giving her trouble. She tried all her tricks, but it was holding fast.

"Hortense!" she said. "I need your help." Hortense held the lock steady while Nana prepared to use the strongest weapon she had: her foot. She slammed it down on the lock. **CLANG!**

"Done!" Nana called, and the other elephants gathered around as she pulled open the gate. "Come out, dear antelopes. You are free!"

Cautiously, a few antelopes wandered out. The first one looked around, bowed its head to the elephants . . . and bolted.

Soon, the other antelopes followed, streaming off into the night until, at last, the pen was empty.

"We did it!" Nana said, and the elephants cheered. Then they heard a noise: Was that a truck? This time, when Nana turned to look, she saw headlights coming their way.

"Run!" Nana trumpeted, and the herd galloped off, the ground shaking beneath their feet.

Once on their home turf and at a safe distance, the elephants huddled together and watched as the vehicle arrived and the people got out to find the pen empty.

Nana turned to Hortense. "I'm sure they meant no harm," she said.

"But wild creatures are just not meant to be penned," Hortense replied. She and Nana smiled at each other in the moonlight.

Life at Thula Thula was good. And certainly not boring.